NERRISA PRATT

Bargello

17 Modern Needlepoint Projects for You and Your Home

Photography by Sarah Hogan

Hardie Grant

QUADRILLE

Contents

Introduction

The Bargello palace in Florence, Italy, is a world-renowned museum, home to works of art by sculptors Michelangelo and Donatello, as well as a collection of colourful textiles and tapestries from Italian history. It was in this museum that historians uncovered an intriguing set of embroidered chairs, thought to be from the 1600s, with a unique hand-worked design that became known as Bargello. Fast-forward a few hundred years, and Bargello was given a new lease of life in the swinging 60s. Throughout the 60s and 70s, Bargello was a fashionable craft that allowed stitchers to create bold interior and fashion design pieces. How-to books from the era show waistcoats and bell bottoms as well as tablecloths and bed linens. Fast-forward another 50 years, and those how-to tomes line my bookshelves, a modern stitcher fascinated by all things Bargello.

My own journey began late one evening a few years ago when, at a loss for a more mindful hobby, I took to Pinterest, the 'go-to' place for any crafter on the search for inspiration. After scrolling through many twee, dated projects, I was frustrated that there didn't seem to be anything for a modern colour-enthuasiast like me. I was just about ready to give up, but then I saw it. Bold lines, geometric shapes and at least three clashing colours, 'Bar-gel-lo' I said out loud to myself. My partner briefly looked up from his laptop, shaking his head at the thought of yet another set of craft supplies taking up space in our flat.

The most exciting thing to me was that I didn't need to wait to get started. I knew that I already had some Aida (the loosely woven fabric used for cross stitch) and a few embroidery threads in my collection, so I got stitching right away. That little cushion took me six months to finish, not for the reasons you might think, but because I took my time and enjoyed each and every stitch. It was mindful crafting at its best. Never before or since have I experienced a craft that you can truly relax with like Bargello. I still have that cushion, and now I smile, looking at the pomegranate shaped stitches. They're all different stitch lengths, and the repeat doesn't line up in the slightest, but I was, and still am, so proud of it.

From a young age, I took an interest in the historical, which eventually followed me into my fashion degree and beyond, into my adult life. I love any excuse to spend spare cash on vintage books, flipping through the pages and experiencing that musty smell only an old book can have. It transports me back to my parents, who had a shared

passion for heritage, taking myself and my little sister to museums. They would take the time to read the descriptions on plaques next to every artefact in the room, encouraging us to take an interest and learn all of their hidden secrets. We would often spend Sundays strolling around National Trust parks in the rain, eating soggy sandwiches thanks to the unpredictable British weather. All the while, mum, a talented artist, would be snapping pictures on a disposable camera, then madly sketching up new ideas as they came to her.

For a long time, Bargello was just something I did in the evenings while binge-watching box sets and drinking back-to-back cups of tea. It wasn't meant to grace the pages of social media; it was just my relaxing, crafty little secret. That was until one day, I finished a piece so perfect, so beautifully colourful, I just had to share it. The reaction really took me by surprise – there were two camps, the 'Wow, what is this crafty magic!?' and the 'Oh my goodness, my mother and grandmother used to Bargello'. I was overwhelmed by the response and decided it would be a great use of my craft teaching experience to show the world how to get stitching.

Today, I run The Bargello Edit, a one-stop shop for supplies, kits and classes designed to bring this retro craft to the modern maker. As charming as 70s Bargello is, I try to inject a more subtle set of colourways into the technique. I also thrive on coming up with exciting, original projects that I love and know other makers will love, too. In fact, the 'Barbara bag', named after my nan, was inspired by the gorgeous designer pieces you see on the runway. Those designer bags might be on-trend, but as with any craft project, you just can't beat the feeling of proudly declaring, 'Yes, I made it!'.

If you're new to Bargello, I'm confident you will fall for it as hard as I have. Once you know the basics, you'll start seeing the world as your canvas, thinking in intricate stitches and clashing colour palettes, really making a mark on your home and your wardrobe, too. Whether you're coming back to Bargello after a few years or you're just looking to have a go at a relaxing, mindful craft, I hope that picking up a needle and canvas is as enjoyable for you as a coffee with an old friend.

SKILL LEVEL KEY

 Beginner

Confident beginner

Intermediate

The Techniques

How to use this book

THE BARGELLO STITCH

The Bargello stitch is beautifully simple to master, and thanks to the very few rules that accompany the craft, once you've grasped the basics, it's easy to develop your personal style. Made up of straight stitches that are determined by their 'length', typically no longer than 5 or 6 squares, patterns and repeats can be created that are as minimal or detailed as you like.

The basic Bargello stitch is simple; each stitch goes into the canvas vertically. To create a triangular shape, you can manipulate your stitches by laying them on the canvas, 'stepping' up or down to produce a balanced shape.

There are a few recognizable variations of the stitch, such as 'Flame stitch' or 'Florentine stitch' as it's also sometimes known. This stitch creates a zig zag pattern for which Bargello tends to be most recognized; you will find multiple variations of this stitch throughout this book as it's an excellent foundation for creating your own patterns and designs.

As well as flame stitch, there are a few recognizable traditional stitches perfect for a beginner to master, such as:

ZIG ZAG

The zig zag stitch is similar to flame stitch in design but has straight lines connecting the peaks and troughs. Play with the scale to create more drama or to showcase a more subtle, tighter set of lines.

HUNGARIAN POINT

This stitch alternates shorter and longer counts to create a stepped pattern. Using a gradient of colours is really effective for this detailed stitch.

SCALLOP

Scallop stitch uses carefully stepped stitches next to one another to create scallops with soft, rounded edges on the canvas.

DIAMONDS

Similar to the triangle, the diamond uses stitches that grow in stitch length as you get to the centre point and then reversed back down in scale to form a diamond.

TRIANGLES

A simple stitch for a beginner, you can use different length stitches to create perfectly even triangles. The upcycled jacket (page 124) uses this technique. Starting small on one side (2 or 3 counts) and gradually get bigger towards the centre, which starts to form the triangle. From there graduate back down to the smallest size again to complete the shape.

CHEVRONS

Chevrons are created using sets of stacked stitches. These stitches can be transformed on the canvas by playing with scale and placement.

CIRCLES

These carefully staggered stitches give the appearance of curves on the canvas.

Supplies

When it comes to creating your own Bargello projects, there are very few materials needed. Here are the essentials you will need to get started. You'll find a couple of extras that are nice to have but not essential for the craft at the end of this list.

TAPESTRY CANVAS
This widely available canvas is perfect for creating softer projects like cushions, clothing or for upholstering furniture. It comes in 'counts', which will denote which size of thread fits best. Traditionally, 10-count paired with a tapestry thread is ideal for most projects.

PLASTIC CANVAS
This rigid canvas is used to create projects with structure and is excellent for beginners as it's sturdy and easy to work with. It comes in sheets of A4 and also has a range of sizes that are commonly referred to as HPI or 'holes per inch'.

NEEDLES
If you're using tapestry wool for a project, a size 18 tapestry needle is essential. It's precisely the right size for the materials and glides effortlessly through the canvas as you stitch. Tapestry needles are blunter than traditional needles, so it's a good idea to have a selection of sharper sewing needles available for constructing projects such as cushions.

CRAFTING SCISSORS
There are two types of scissors you need for any Bargello project. The first is a pair of crafting scissors. As you'll be using these to cut either type of canvas, you need to ensure these are nice and sharp so your cuts are accurate.

EMBROIDERY SNIPS
These scissors will be your constant companion throughout your projects, so choose a pair that you find easy to operate. Spring-loaded snips are more expensive but make quick work of a snip at the end of a row of stitches.

MEASURING TAPE/RULER
When it comes to creating accurate finished projects, a ruler is vital to ensure they fit together to the nearest millimetre. As plastic canvas can differ ever so slightly between manufacturers, it's always best to measure and then count the number of squares as well.

NOTEBOOK
There are lots of numbers involved in Bargello, from remembering the colour codes for the threads used to the counts and steps for each of your projects. It's a good idea to have a dedicated notebook so that you can record all the details of your makes in case you ever want to recreate them.

GRAPH PAPER
Once you've got the basics of Bargello down, you may want to begin designing your own unique patterns and repeats. There are several ways to do this, but a simple and cost-effective method is to use graph paper to plot out your designs. Use each square on the paper to represent a square on your project, so you can make sure patterns work before you take a needle to your canvas.

MASKING TAPE
For projects on canvas, it's always best to prep the edges of your canvas with masking tape to ensure you don't lose the edge of your project to any fraying.

SOLUBLE PEN
This is great for marking up your canvas projects without leaving a lasting mark. A Sharpie is equally as good on a plastic canvas.

BULLDOG CLIPS
When it comes to seaming projects on a plastic grid together, it can sometimes feel like you need a few extra hands. Using a bulldog clip is a great way to secure your project without damaging your stitches.

PINS
A crafter's essential. A set of good pins will help when constructing fabric projects to ensure the finish is as accurate as possible.

SEWING MACHINE *(nice to have)*
Although not essential, a sewing machine is a quick and efficient way to finish up your textile projects. Most of the projects in this book can be hand sewn, but a sewing machine will ensure you have a professional, durable finish so you can use your project for years to come.

LAP FRAME *(nice to have)*
Traditionally, Bargello is worked on a hoop or a frame like traditional embroidery. If you're finding a particular part of a design challenging, you may find that a lap frame could help you manoeuvre your piece more easily.

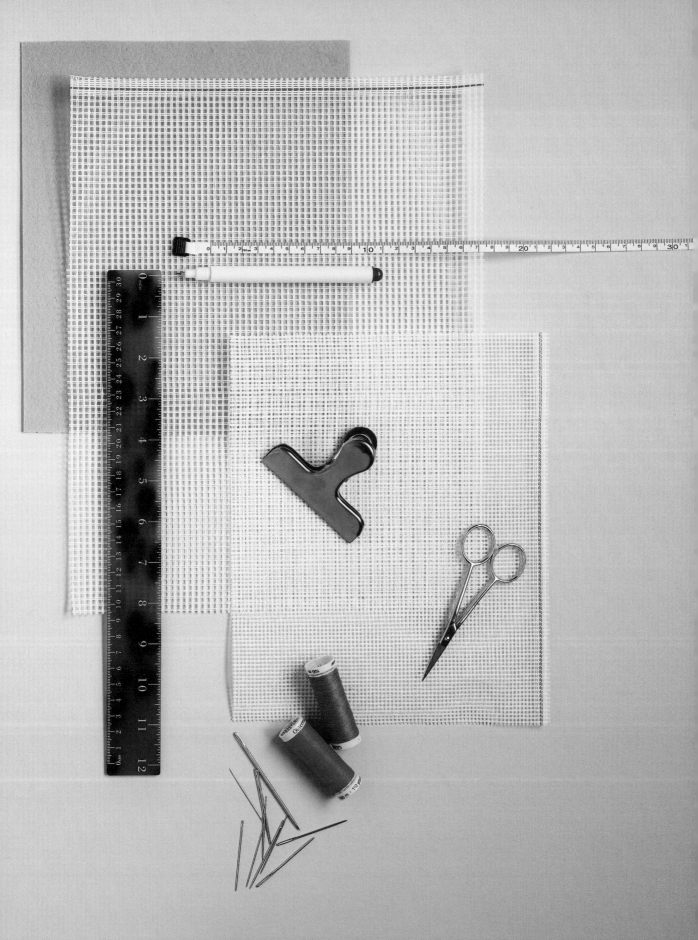

Preparing the canvas

Before starting a project, make sure your canvas is prepped and ready. This will make it easier to work on the design and help you achieve the best result on your finished project. Since we'll mainly be working with fabric and plastic canvas in this book, here are the ways you can prepare them both.

FABRIC CANVAS

This type of canvas probably needs the most preparation out of the two as you'll find the canvas will both soften and fray as you stitch. Failure to prepare this canvas could result in you not being able to complete your design.

1 To prepare your fabric canvas, decide on the size of the finished project and mark this on the canvas using a water-soluble marker. Then add a healthy seam allowance of 1.5–2cm (⅝–¾in) to your outline and mark this on the canvas, creating a frame. Once you have done this, rearrange to cut out your project using the seam allowance border as a guide.

2 To prepare the canvas for stitching, you will need to secure the edges. You can use masking tape or any other low-tack tape for this. Simply fold the tape around the edges, ensuring they'll be protected as your arm brushes past them repeatedly. This tape can also be a handy place to make notes on important things like measurements and thread colour codes used, so you can remind yourself at a glance without needing to dig out your notebook.

PLASTIC CANVAS

There isn't much prep required from a plastic canvas other than to double-check you're working with the right size and count. If you're unsure of which size canvas you have in your stash, you can take a ruler and count how many holes there are within 2.5cm (1in). This is key as a 10-count from one brand can differ ever so slightly from another.

1 Mark your plastic canvas using a marker pen and ruler. It's advisable to count the squares along the length and width of the canvas, as well as using the measurements. This is particularly important for projects that have more than one panel or section that need to be identical – while a ruler is useful, if the measurement falls between squares, it can be hard to see such a tiny anomaly by eye. The difference of one square between panels or sections could affect the whole project.

2 Cut out your canvas with regular crafting scissors.

The foundation stitch

As you begin to Bargello, you'll see that your eye begins to follow the repeat pattern easily once you have a solid foundation in place, and progress will become relatively quick. Try to get into the habit of working the same way with all projects, starting in the bottom left-hand corner and working across the canvas from left to right, filling the canvas with stitches from the bottom to the top.

To start a foundation stitch, take a look at your pattern and find the first full repeat. This is the set of stitches that can be put on the canvas with no breaks or with shorter stitch lengths than the pattern determines.

Once you have identified the first full repeat, stitch onto the canvas, completing the line in full. You now have your foundation stitch in place. Now you can begin to lay your stitched pattern above, filling the canvas all the way to the top. Should there be any space under the foundation stitch, fill this at the end, using leftover scraps of wool to fill the gaps.

Threading the needle

When it comes to threading the needle, working with a thread that has multiple strands can be tricky as you don't want to split them and ruin your fibres. This simple method will ensure they remain intact:

1 Take a small piece of paper (the bands around DMC and Anchor threads work really well for this) and fold it in half. Score the fold gently with your nail.

2 Snip the piece of paper so that it's around 5mm (¼in) in width and 6cm (2⅜in) in length. You should now have a small piece of paper with a fold running lengthways.

3 Open up the piece of paper and place the tail end of the wool inside, then close the paper, sandwiching the thread in between.

4 Holding it tightly, shimmy the folded edge of the paper through the eye of the needle, bringing the thread through at the same time.

For all projects, try to keep thread lengths no longer than your forearm. The thread will travel through the canvas multiple times as you stitch, and the longer the piece, the more threadbare it will look towards the end.

Another handy tip when it comes to thread is to have two piles when you work: a scraps pile for unusable threads that are too tiny to stitch with and a pile of threads you can use again. Bargello can be really low-waste if you use your threads wisely.

The basic stitch using the 'no knot' method

Unlike other types of embroidery, for Bargello projects, we avoid the use of knots. This is to ensure your stitches sit nice and flat, resulting in a neat and consistent finish across your work. Knots would also make it easy to accidentally knock or pull out your work as you create your project due to the delicate stacking up of stitches and colours.

Without a knot, it can seem a little daunting getting started on a piece, but it's actually very simple (see photographs on pages 24–25):

Securing the start
1 Thread your needle. Come up through the canvas in your starting position and pull through.

2 As the thread end reduces to around 2.5cm (1in), stop and hold this in place under the canvas between your thumb and finger.

3 Finish your stitch, coming back through the canvas, holding the tail end tight as you do. Move on to the next stitch, coming up through your canvas as before. As you come back down, manoeuvre the tail end, so it begins to be covered by the stitches.

4 Continue stitching, and after 3 or 4 stitches, you'll see that the thread disappears, and everything is securely in place on the canvas. Continue working.

To cover the thread ends on the back of your canvas, all of your stitches must be consistent. If you're moving up the canvas, start at the bottom of the stitch and come back through the top. As you move down the canvas, do the reverse, starting at the top of your stitch, coming back through the canvas at the bottom.

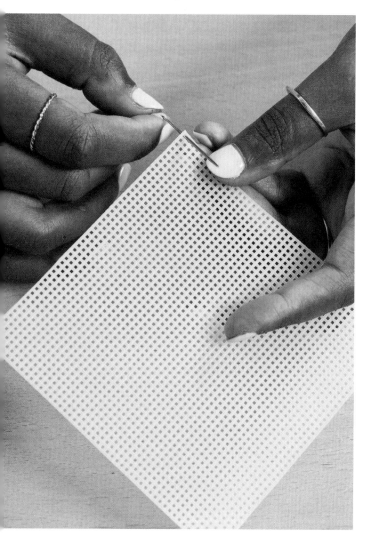

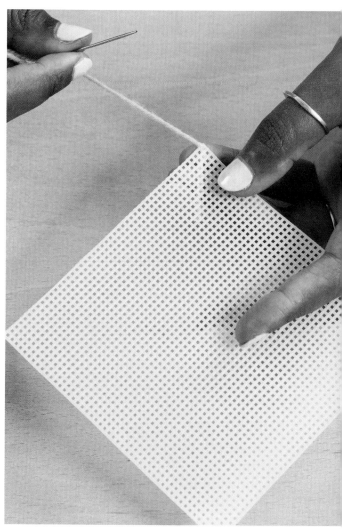

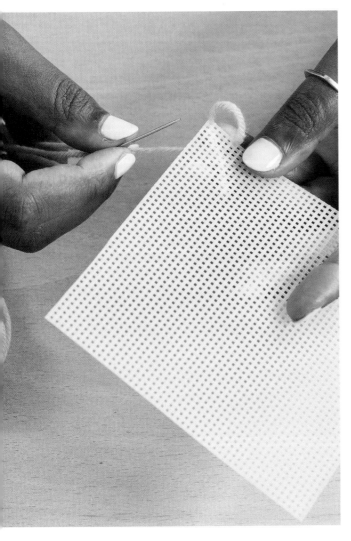

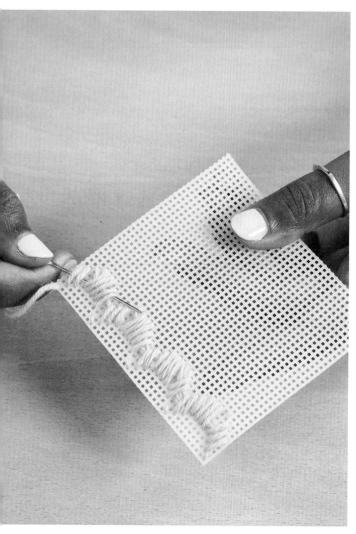

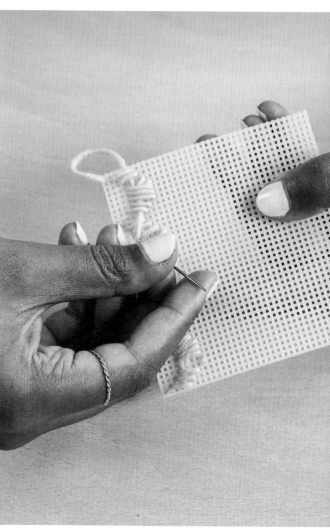

Finishing a thread

As you will be working with shorter yarn lengths, it will be common for you to run out of thread a few times per row. Finishing a thread and adding a new one is simple:

1 When you have 4–5cm (1.5–2in) of thread left, run the needle underneath the stitches on the reverse of the canvas; 2.5cm (1in) will be more than enough. Then snip the remaining thread away.

2 As a rule, if you're not sure if you have enough thread left to finish, it's best to check you can still comfortably manoeuvre the needle without the thread slipping from the eye of the needle.

Adding a new thread

1 Once you've finished, you'll need to add more working thread to your project so you can continue stitching. To begin, thread your needle as before.

2 Working towards where you'll make your next stitch, slip the needle under the threads on the reverse just as you did before. Use your thumb and forefinger to secure it in place.

3 Hold it in place for one or two stitches just to ensure you don't pull the thread all of the way through. Now that the new length of thread is in place as you begin stitching again.

It's important to note that once you've followed the 'no knot' method, you won't need to do it again on your canvas. Instead, follow the instructions for adding in new colours on pages 28–29, to continue with the rest of your stitches.

Adding in new colours

Bargello is full of wonderful colour combinations and clashing palettes, and so, of course, there's absolutely no doubt you'll want to add a new colour (or three!) as you stitch. To do this:

1 Using the row below, gently slip your needle under the stitches on the reverse of the canvas.

2 Thread you needle through the existing stitches, towards where you want to begin your next set of stitches.

3 In most cases, as you start stitching, your first stitch in the count will share a hole with the square below. This will ensure the canvas is brimming full of stitches and there are no gaps.

4 Come up through the canvas and start your new row of stitches, holding the thread in place with your thumb and finger.

5 Work a few stitches to ensure everything is secure and then continue as normal.

6 Finish your thread as instructed on page 27.

>> 1 <<

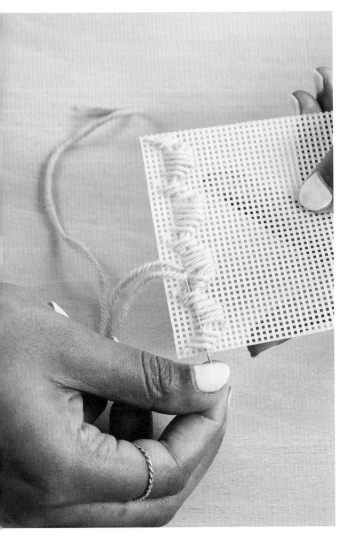

>> 2 <<

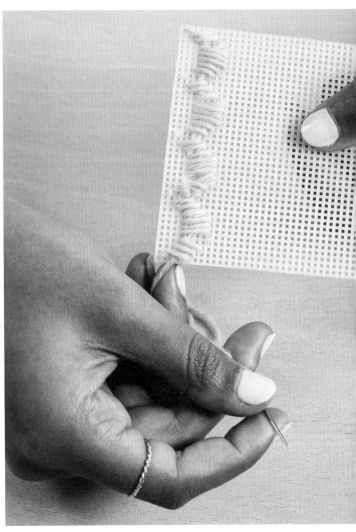

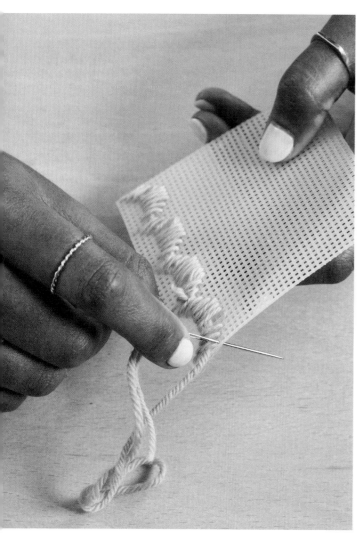

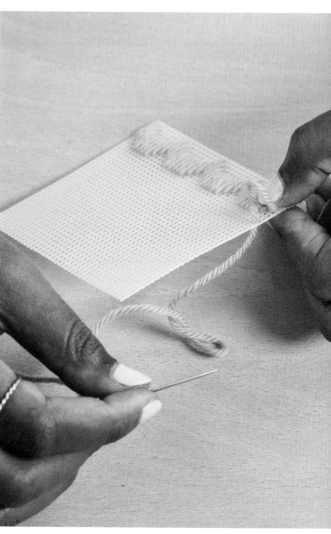

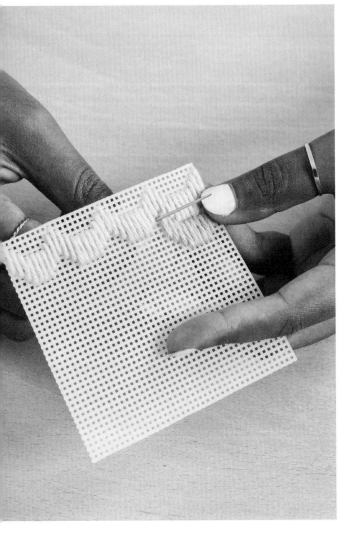

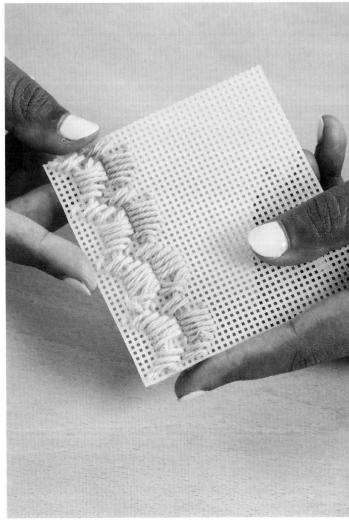

Reading a chart

Like most hand-stitching crafts, Bargello has a range of patterns and charts that are perfect for beginners. In Bargello, a pattern is repeated until the canvas is full, so these may look a little different to charts you've seen before. Here's a breakdown of what to expect from a Bargello pattern:

CANVAS SIZE

This refers to the canvas or grid you'll need to work with to recreate the project. These can be adapted, but bear in mind that adapting the scale could produce a different overall effect.

STITCH LENGTH/COUNTS

Describes how many squares your needle needs to jump over before going back through the canvas. Depending on the pattern, this can be referred to as the stitch length or the count.

STEP UP/DOWN

This tells the maker how many squares to move up or down the grid for the next stitch. This is important as stepping up or down by too many or two few squares can throw your whole project off.

PATTERN

A Bargello pattern isn't usually the entire project on a chart like a traditional embroidery pattern. Instead, it's a section of the design and requires the user to repeat this on the canvas until it's full. More often than not, it'll show the first full repeat, which is useful for plotting your foundation stitch onto the canvas.

ARROWS

The arrows indicate the centre point of your design, making it easier to locate the middle of your design on your canvas or grid.

Designing your own patterns

Once you've mastered the basics of Bargello, chances are you'll want to branch out and start creating your own patterns. There are so many variations to be created, but sometimes when you start stitching, the vision in your head isn't reflected on the canvas in front of you.

A simple piece of graph paper and some colourful fine liners are a great way to plot out your patterns before you get stuck in. Think of the squares on the paper as the squares on your canvas. You can play with pattern and scale to make sure everything lines up before you really get stuck in. Here are some tips to get started:

START SMALL
First, try creating your pattern repeat on a small grid that represents your design to really focus on the details.

PLOT THE DESIGN
Once you're happy with the design, cut a piece of graph paper in a similar size to your finished project. If you need a larger piece of graph paper, you can easily tape the sheets of an A4 pad together. Alternatively, it can be purchased in rolls.

Take the small pattern repeat you created and work it across the paper, ensuring the repeat works in multiples. Make any changes before you commit to a final design.

Traditionally, Bargello patterns are created using 3 colours repeated to build up the retro palettes and styles you may have seen in old books. However, I firmly believe that as long as your colours are balanced and symmetrical, you can really have a play and create modern variations on the designs that I know you'll just love.

Swatching

Swatching is an essential part of the Bargello process. Some larger pieces of Bargello take days or even weeks, so you don't want to get halfway through and realize your colour palette doesn't work or there is a mistake in your repeat.

Making smaller swatches of your work is a great way to test your designs and uses up any scraps you might have. Keep any pieces that are big enough in your craft stash, and you'll never be short of sampling material.

CREATING A SWATCH

1 Cut your chosen material to size. Depending on the project, these can be between 7–10cm (3–4in) square.

2 Using your design, start stitching the small section onto the canvas. As you go, ensure your pattern works and adapt the stitches if required. Transfer any changes made to the paper pattern.

3 Pay attention to the colour palette. Does it work as you planned? If not, now is a great time to make any tweaks.

4 If you have a few colour palettes in mind, don't be afraid to make a few swatches. More often than not, once you're done, the one you love most will jump out at you.

5 Once you've completed a swatch, it's always good to record what you used and when. Either make a note in your dedicated Bargello notebook or put a sticky label on the back. Be sure to include details like the thread manufacturer and colour codes, too.

Calculating thread quantities

Depending on your pattern, swatching can be a great way to predict the quantity of materials you'll need. To do this:

1 Use a ruler to measure out a length of thread; 30cm (12in) is a good length to work with. Thread your needle.

2 Begin stitching as normal. As you run low on thread, measure another length and have a notebook nearby to record a tally every time you add a new thread length of 30cm (12in).

3 Work this way with all of the colours in your repeat. When you are finished, tally up how much of each thread colour you used. You may use some colours more than once in the pattern, so it's important to factor this in.

4 Take the colour you used the most and add up the total thread used. Multiply this number by the size of your actual project. For example, if your sample is 10x10cm (4x4in), but your finished piece will be 30x30cm (12x12in), you can multiply how much thread was used by 9 (as 9 10x10cm squares go into a 30x30cm square) to get the approximate amount you will need.

5 It's always advisable to add a few metres (yards) to this amount to allow for mistakes and waste.

Picking colours

One of the best parts of a project, choosing your colour palette is a chance to be creative and inject your own style into the design. As Bargello is so unapologetically bright and fun, there are many colour options (sometimes too many!). Here are a few approaches to picking colours to make sure all your palettes live in perfect harmony:

GRADIENTS
Many traditional Bargello projects use gradients to create harmony. Starting with your favourite colour, slightly graduate the colour into lighter or darker shades as you move up the canvas to create a beautiful effect without adding too many clashing shades to the mix. If you're feeling braver, try blocking your gradients to create multi-tonal stripes on your project.

CLASHING COLOURS
Probably one of my favourites. There are always those shades that shouldn't look good together but do. Combinations like pink and green or lilac and rust, work really well together if you keep the rest of the palette neutral. Don't introduce too many other colours into the mix. For my own process, I have a small swatch of each thread colour stitched onto canvas, which I like to play around with when developing new projects. This is not only satisfying if, like me, you love organized crafting, but it's also a great way to add and remove colours.

INSPIRATION
When designing a project for your home, you'll already have an idea of the space that you want the final piece to live in. Take a look around that room and think about the colours and tones that are already in play. Perhaps there is a bold wallpaper with a beautiful colour palette, or you might already have some cushions in varying shades that this project could coordinate with.

PINTEREST
It goes without saying that Pinterest is a gold mine for inspiration, and Bargello is no exception. From fashion collections to interiors and even other crafts, Pinterest is brimming with colour palette ideas.

MOODBOARDS
There are potential projects to be seen all around us, so don't be afraid to go back to basics with your inspiration. Tear palettes from magazines or print them out from your digital scrapbook. Try layering up images and threads on paper to conjure up new ideas. You can even add your test swatches and potential thread choices into the mix, creating a library of references for future projects.

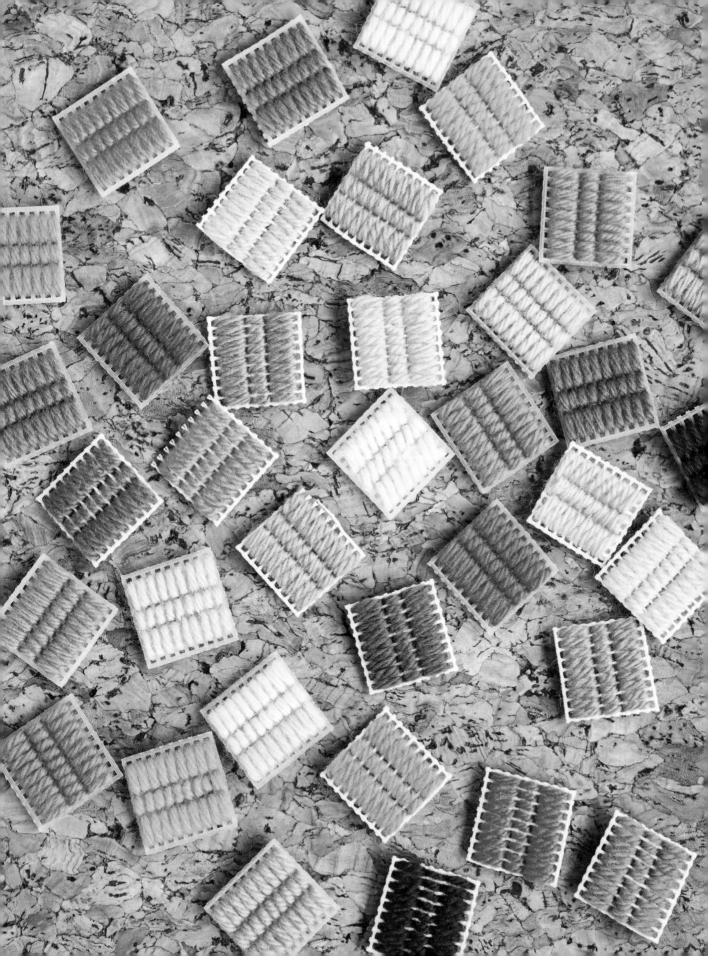

Perfect pairings

When my journey with Bargello began, there was absolutely no wait time between me discovering the craft and getting started on my first project as I had materials at home. I think this is true for most crafters as we tend to have stashes that could rival a craft store. Before you get started, take a look at this list of materials that work well together. You might find that you already have some items in your stash and only need to purchase one or two additional items. As well as the traditional pairings, you'll quickly start to see potential compatible canvas and thread combinations as you work through the projects in this book.

Although there are traditional materials that Bargello is known for, it pays to experiment. I've played with alternative materials over the years, allowing me to work on projects using products I already have in my craft room, saving me money and helping me to avoid creating waste by stocking up on excess materials.

10-COUNT CANVAS/PLASTIC GRID AND TAPESTRY WOOL/CHUNKY YARN

This is perhaps the most common pairing. Tapestry yarn is available in a huge range of shades, and stitches created using this yarn lay flat and evenly on 10-count canvas. When it comes to canvas choice, there are two options I recommend: tapestry canvas for textile projects and plastic grid for more structured pieces.

7-COUNT CANVAS/PLASTIC GRID AND SUPER-CHUNKY YARN

This pairing is fantastic for little hands or hesitant beginners. With larger-scale materials, it's quicker and easier to see your progress on the canvas as you learn the basics. As with most materials, this comes as a tapestry canvas or plastic grid option.

14-COUNT CANVAS/PLASTIC GRID AND STRANDED COTTON/EMBROIDERY FLOSS

One of my favourite pairings, this combination makes clean, perfect stitches that translate into premium looking projects like the letter patch on page 129 or the headband on page 134.

The Projects

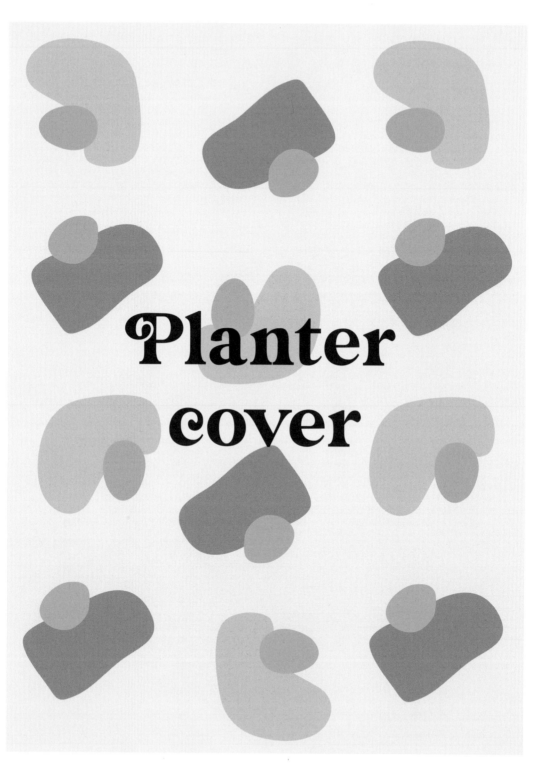

Planter cover

Add a touch of colour to your plant collection with this simple project, perfect for Bargello beginners. Using a simple curved pattern, mix and match your colours to complement the other pots in your collection or really create a standout piece with clashing shades.

PATTERN
Scallop

MATERIALS
10-count plastic grid
Tapestry wool in 5 colours
Size 18 tapestry needle
Bulldog clip (optional)
Paper
Pen or pencil
Ruler

SKILLS
Drafting a planter pattern
Stitching with plastic grid
Following a pattern
Seaming panels

METHOD

1 Measure the diameter of your nursery pot. Using a ruler, draw a line the same length vertically on a piece of paper.

2 Mark the halfway point along this line and draw another line the same length through the centre, making a cross on the page.

3 Measure the distance between two of the cross ends and mark the paper at the halfway point. Repeat until you have the original cross on the page with a small mark in the centre of each segment.

4 Using your ruler, draw a line through the middle of the 'X' using the marks you just made to make sure it's straight. Next, join all of the lines together on the outer edge to create an octagon.

5 To ensure your planter is even, measure the end of each segment and make a note of the widths on the paper to keep track. Once you've checked them all, calculate the average width and make a note of the final measurement.

6 Take the height of your nursery pot and mark this on your paper. You may want to add 1–2cm (⅜–¾in) to ensure the pot is fully covered.

7 Now cut your panels to size, using the height and average width of each segment to make a rectangular panel. For this project, you'll need eight panels. If you're drafting a bigger or smaller pot, you may want to add more or less, but this will depend on the desired effect.

8 Follow the chart opposite to stitch your pattern onto the panels, one by one, making sure to regularly check the ends of all the lines match up when you place the panels side by side.

9 Once you've completed all eight panels, we're going to 'seam' the project together. To do this, take two panels with right sides facing up and line them up so the stitched edges all match up row for row. Use the bulldog clip to secure the panels in place.

10 Thread your needle in the colour of your choice. Starting with the centre seam, insert your needle under the stitches at the bottom of the two panels. We're going to work our way up to the bulldog clip.

11 Come up through the canvas, gently nudging the stitches closest to the edge out of the way as you do so. Then pull the needle through gently. Jump over to the adjacent square on the second panel. As before, nudge the stitches out of the way and come back down through the canvas.

12 Repeat all the way to the top. Take care to keep the panels lined up as you go so you don't bend the canvas out of shape.

13 Once you've joined two panels together, continue to add more panels one by one. Connect each of the panels to the edge of another and stitch a centre seam to connect them. Keep going until you have one long set of panels.

14 Then, starting from the left-hand side, we're going to edge stitch the canvas using the finishing technique on page 27. When you come to a centre seam, create a 'fake stitch' in the middle of the join to make sure there are no gaps on the finished project.

15 Once both edges are finished, join the sides of your planter together. To do this, we will use the same technique as above. Secure the end panels together using a bulldog clip (don't worry if you need to flatten the planter to do this). Stitch up the centre seam as before, then secure the thread by weaving it back under the edge stitching.

>> **9** <<

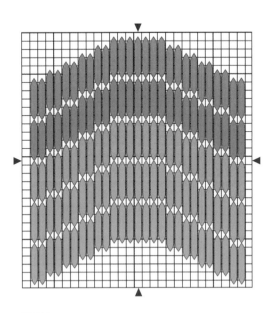

KEY

Light pink (7151)

Dark pink (7605)

Orange (7436)

Yellow (7058)

Tan (7453)

COUNT
6

STEP
1

Trinket dish

SKILL LEVEL  10 HOURS +

Keep your dressing table tidy and your trinkets safe with this simple yet intricate project. Level up your skills by adding a pre-drilled wooden base. Once you've created one, why not play with different shapes and sizes to create a whole host of storage dishes?

PATTERN
Zig zag

MATERIALS
10-count plastic grid
Tapestry wool in 3 colours
Size 18 tapestry needle
Measuring tape
Pre-drilled wooden base
Bulldog clip (optional)

SKILLS
Stitching with plastic grid
Following a pattern
Adding a wooden base

METHOD

1 Start by measuring the circumference of your chosen base. Make a note of this measurement, as this will be the length of your canvas.

2 Next, decide on the depth you'd like the dish to be. Cut a piece of plastic canvas using your length and depth measurements. If you're using a normal sheet of 10-count plastic grid, you will likely need to cut two separate pieces. To do this, simply divide the length in half.

3 Following the chart on page 56, stitch your pattern onto the grid. Once complete, if necessary, seam any separate pieces together along the horizontal edges (see page 50).

4 Finish both the top and the bottom of the panels using the edge stitch.

5 Seam the final side together, creating a complete loop.

6 To attach the canvas to the base, place the loop of canvas over the top of the base and shimmy it down as far as it will go. For the finish to work, you'll need to ensure the bottom edge of the base and the canvas line up.

7 Take a length of wool and thread your needle. Close to one of the pre-drilled holes on the base, pass your needle under the stitches on the canvas in a downward direction. Pass the wool under the base.

8 Gently come up through the base
and loop around to the Bargello piece,
pushing the needle through your stitches
again to secure everything in place.

9 Now jump to the next pre-drilled hole.
Come up through the base and weave
your needle through your stitches to
secure the two together.

10 Repeat until the base is completely
attached – you may want to repeat this
step to add decorative stitches to the
inside of the dish.

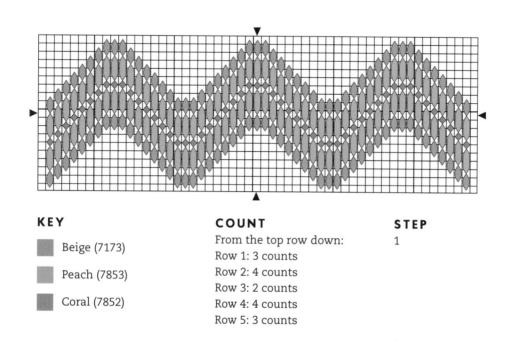

KEY

Beige (7173)

Peach (7853)

Coral (7852)

COUNT

From the top row down:
Row 1: 3 counts
Row 2: 4 counts
Row 3: 2 counts
Row 4: 4 counts
Row 5: 3 counts

STEP

1

>> **8** <<

Upcycled lampshade

Rattan furniture is a classic way to add a touch of retro-chic styling to your interiors. Breathe new life into a pre-loved piece by adding some simple stitches in neutral tones.

PATTERN
Zig zag

MATERIALS
Rattan lampshade
Raffia yarn in 2 colours
Darning needle

SKILLS
Stitching on an alternative canvas
Following a pattern

METHOD

1 To begin your project, thread your needle with a length of raffia: work with a longer length so you can double this over to really fill the squares.

2 Come up through the lampshade and stitch over your yarn end. This is a little trickier with raffia so take your time to achieve a neat finish.

3 For every stitch you work, go back and ensure the stitches are flat and full. You can use your fingers to 'fluff' the threads and make them look fuller, if necessary.

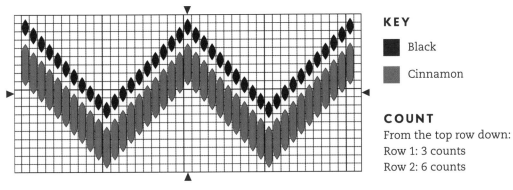

KEY

■ Black

■ Cinnamon

COUNT
From the top row down:
Row 1: 3 counts
Row 2: 6 counts

STEP
1

Wall hanging

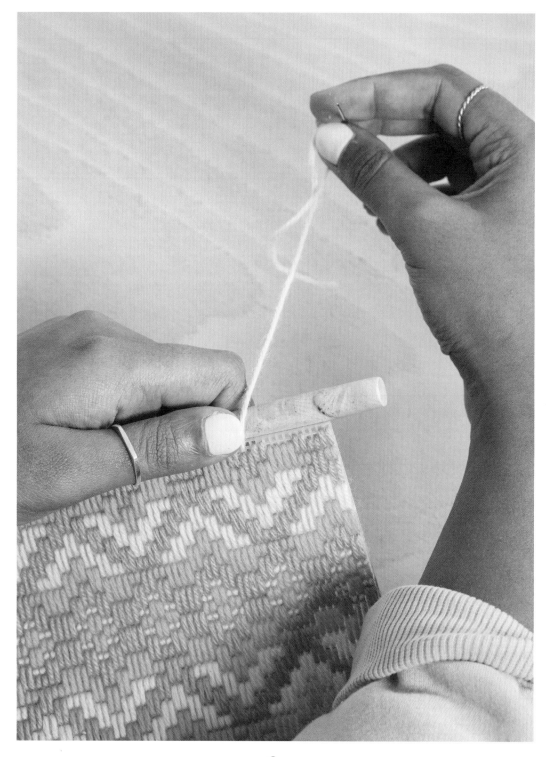

>> **9** <<

Add a pop of colour to your gallery wall with this modern update on a retro wall hanging. Take a closer look to see the abstract hearts hidden in the design. Skill wise, use this project to master the art of on-trend fringing.

PATTERN
Mirrored hearts

MATERIALS
10-count plastic grid
Tapestry wool in 3 colours
Size 18 tapestry needle
Bulldog clip (optional)
Macramé hanging dowel
Macramé cord

SKILLS
Stitching with plastic grid
Following a pattern
Adding a fringe

METHOD

1 For this project, we're going to use a whole sheet of plastic grid to create a statement wall hanging. Take a piece of 10-count plastic grid and simply snip the hanger off the top.

2 Before beginning, we're going to stitch a 'foundation', and as this project will have a large repeat, we'll break it down by colour. It'll make things much easier on your eyes to work this way and ensure you don't go wrong with your stitches.

3 Starting at the bottom of the grid, follow the pattern on page 69 with your main thread colour (in this project I used pink) but leave the first three rows of squares blank at the base. The empty squares will give us space to add the fringe at the end of the project.

4 Fill your canvas with the hearts from the design; this should fill the grid in one colour. Keep an eye out for the change in stitch counts in some parts of the pattern.

5 As you near the top of the canvas, skip the four consecutive stitches on the pattern. These will help to form spaces for the decorative stitches when we attach the hanging dowel.

6 With your foundation complete, you can begin filling in the gaps with the next two colours. Following the pattern closely, once again work with one colour at a time until complete. Note the stitch count changes as before, so make sure you take your time and double-check as you go.

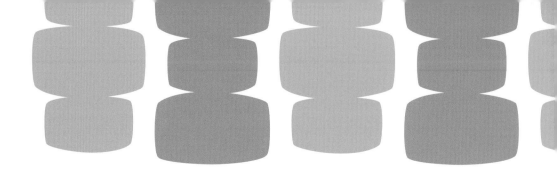

7 Once the canvas is complete, we're going to add the dowel. Take a bulldog clip or similar and use it to secure the dowel in place along the top edge of the canvas. Make sure you're happy with the position of the dowel before you begin stitching.

8 Thread your needle and run your thread under the top row of stitches, towards the left-hand side of the canvas.

9 Come up from underneath the canvas and loop around the dowel until you can push the needle through where the pattern stitches ended. There shouldn't be any gaps.

10 Repeat until the dowel is completely covered and secured in place. You will need to rethread the needle a few times as you do this.

11 To add the fringe, cut 25cm (10in) lengths of wool. For this project, there are a total of 54 individual strands in one row, so ensure you have enough wool to fill the canvas.

12 To add a piece of fringe, fold your thread in half lengthways. Then, using the needle threading method, place both ends inside a folded piece of paper and pass them through the eye of the needle at the same time.

13 Next, go down through the canvas. Come back up through the closest hole to the right but don't pull this all the way through. You should be left with a loop.

14 Guide your needle through the loop and pull the knot tight. You can remove the needle as you do this. Repeat in each 4-square space until all the squares are full.

15 Finally, you will need to add some thread to the macramé dowel to hang your piece. Depending on the style you're going for, you can use the same tapestry wool you've used throughout the project or add some macramé cord for a bolder finish.

>> **14** <<

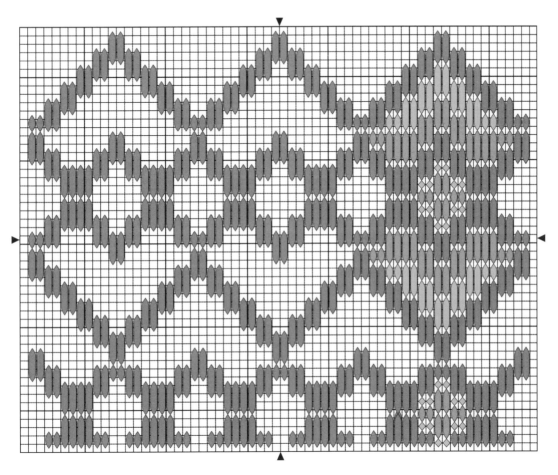

KEY

■ Dark pink (7605)

■ Orange (7436)

■ Beige (7500)

COUNT

Heart outline: 5 counts
Heart centre joins: 3 counts
Middle detail: 2, 3 and 4
counts – see chart for
more detail

STEP

3

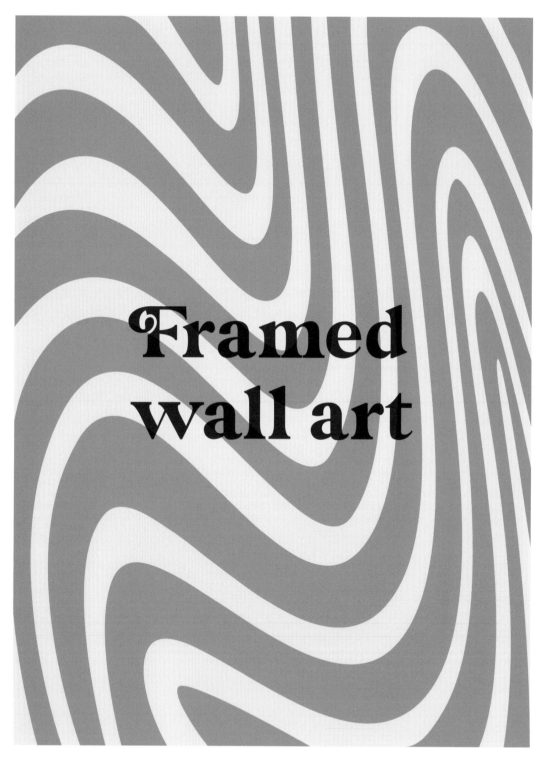

Framed wall art

SKILL LEVEL

 5 HOURS +

For a more minimal take on the wall hanging design, this project uses the same pattern to create a framed piece of Bargello art. Create a set in your favourite colours to tie your Bargello into your décor.

PATTERN
Mirrored hearts

MATERIALS
10-count plastic grid
DK yarn in 3 colours
Size 18 tapestry needle
3cm (1¼in) deep box
    frame 20x20cm (8x8in)

SKILLS
Stitching with plastic grid
Following a pattern

METHOD

1 Take your frame and measure a piece of 10-count plastic canvas the same size.

2 Before beginning, we're going to stitch a 'foundation', and as this project will have a large repeat, we'll break it down by colour. This will make things easier on your eyes and ensure you don't go wrong with your stitches.

3 Starting at the bottom of the grid, follow the pattern on page 74. Fill your canvas with just the hearts from the design, this should fill the grid in the main colour (for this project I used vintage pink), be sure to keep an eye on the change from 5 counts to 3 in some parts of the pattern. With the foundation complete, fill the design with the other two colours. Keep an eye out for the change in stitch counts in some areas of the pattern

4 To finish the project, take the box frame and place your design inside. You can add a mount to the piece, if desired.

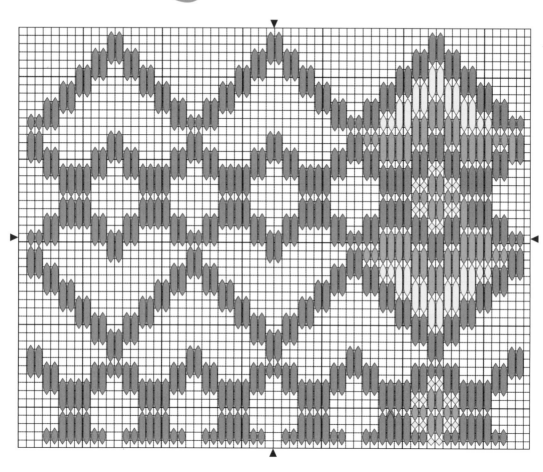

KEY

■ Vintage pink (155)

■ Melon (116)

▢ Granite grey (106)

COUNT

Heart outline: 5 counts
Heart centre joins: 3 counts
Middle detail: 2, 3 and 4
counts – see chart for
more detail

STEP

2

>> **4** <<

Upcycled furniture

SKILL LEVEL

 1 HOUR

>> 1 <<

>> 2 <<

Add a unique geometric detail to existing homewares with this simple project. Rattan furniture is the perfect alternative canvas for Bargello; keep an eye out in charity shops for any bargains that you could upcycle.

PATTERN
Diamonds

MATERIALS
Rattan furniture
Raffia yarn in 2 colours
Darning needle

SKILLS
Stitching on alternative canvas
Following a pattern

METHOD

1 To begin your project, thread your needle with a length of raffia, work with a longer length so you can double this over to really fill the squares.

2 Come up through the rattan and stitch over your yarn end. This can be a little trickier with raffia than with yarn, so take your time.

3 Follow the chart below. After every stitch, go back and ensure it is sitting flat and is nice and full. You can use your fingers to 'fluff' the threads a little if need be.

NOTE
Optional, to protect your stitches cut a piece of adhesive felt to size and place it over the back of the panel to keep them in place.

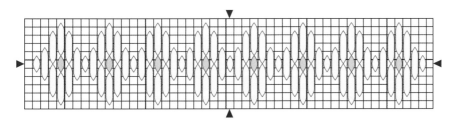

KEY

☐ Ivory white

▨ Desert palm

COUNT
From left to right:
3 counts, 5 counts
Centre stitch 3 counts

STEP
From to left to right:
1 step, 2 steps, 1 steps

Square cushion

SKILL LEVEL

 10 HOURS +

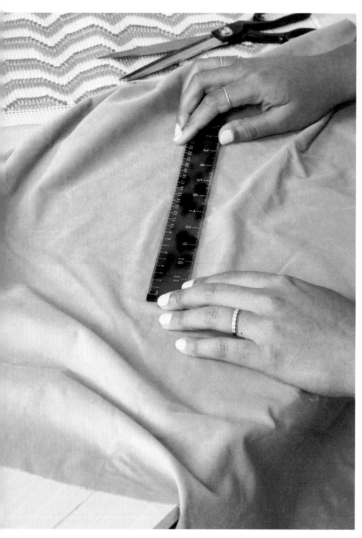

You can never have too many cushions! This project is not only perfect for beginners but also adds a welcome palette of modern colours and simple lines to your home. Coordinate the colours with your current cushion collection or go bold and create a stand out piece. This project makes a 40x40cm (16x16in) cushion cover but could easily be made bigger or smaller depending on your space.

PATTERN
Hungarian Point

MATERIALS
7-count tapestry canvas
Chunky yarn in 4 colours
Size 18 tapestry needle
Backing fabric 50x50cm (20x20in)
42cm (16½in) zip
Cushion inner 40x40cm (16x16in)

SKILLS
Stitching with tapestry canvas
Following a pattern
Adding a cushion back

METHOD

1 Stitch the design onto your canvas, following the pattern on page 84.

2 Once you've completed your Bargello masterpiece, it's time to finish the project by adding a back cover with a zip. To do this, pick your fabric of choice and measure out a 42x48cm (16½x18⅞in) rectangle. Mark each corner using chalk or a washable marker and then connect them to create the rectangle.

3 Draw a line directly through the middle of the rectangle vertically on the longest side, so you have two 42x24cm (16½x9½in) rectangles.

4 Using a pair of fabric scissors, cut your rectangles out, so you have two identical shapes.

5 Fold the fabric on the longest edge over to the wrong side by 2cm (¾in) and press in place. With the right sides facing up, pin the folded edge of the fabric as close to the zip teeth as you can.

6 Repeat on the second piece of fabric.

7 Use a sewing machine (or a needle and thread) stitch the zip in place securely.

8 With the zip closed three quarters of the way, pin the cushion back and the finished Bargello piece together with right sides facing. Take your time to make sure everything lines up equally.

9 Stitch around all four edges to attach the back and front pieces together. Make sure your zip is partially open when you do this so you can get open it fully once you have stitched it up.

10 Trim the seam allowances and snip the corners diagonally as close to the stitches as you can.

11 Slide the partially open zip all the way open and turn the cushion the right way out. Use closed scissors to push the corners out into neat points.

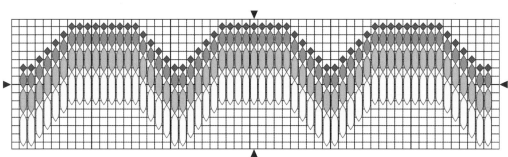

KEY		COUNT	STEP
■	Teal (1062)	From the top to the bottom:	1
■	Pale rose (1080)	Row 1: 2 counts	
■	Mustard (1823)	Row 2: 3 counts	
□	White (1005)	Row 3: 4 counts	
		Row 4: 5 counts	

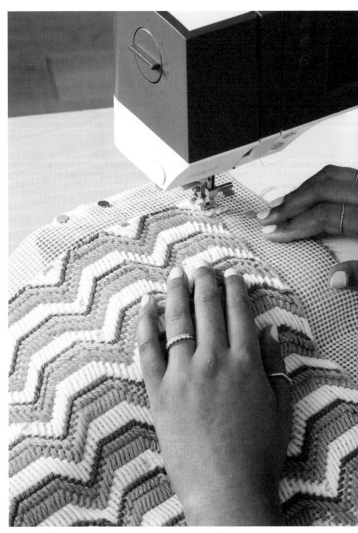

Oblong cushion

SKILL LEVEL

 10 HOURS +

4

A modern twist on a Bargello cushion. This minimal project is all about laying a foundation in a neutral shade and then using a simple formula of repeated colours to fill in the gaps.

PATTERN
Chevron

MATERIALS
10-count tapestry canvas
Tapestry wool in 4 colours
Size 18 tapestry needle
Backing fabric 30x45cm (12x16in)
42cm (16½in) zip

SKILLS
Stitching with tapestry canvas
Following a pattern
Adding a cushion back

METHOD

1 For this project, you will need to fill your canvas with the 'grid' first so that you can fill it in once you have a repeat pattern. To do this, follow the foundation stitch first in the main colour; in this case, it's all of the cream stitches. Once the foundation is in place, you can begin to fill in the gaps using the following combinations: green (5 stitches), blue (4 stitches), lilac (6 stitches).

2 Finish the project by adding a back cover with a zip. To do this, measure out a 25x45cm (10x17¾in) rectangle. Mark each corner using chalk or a washable marker and then connect them to create the rectangle.

3 Draw a line directly through the middle of the rectangle vertically on the longest side, so you have two 45x12.5cm (16x9in) rectangles.

4 Using a pair of fabric scissors, cut your rectangles out, so you have two identical shapes.

5 Fold the fabric on the longest edge over to the wrong side by 2cm (¾in) and press in place. With the right sides facing up, pin the folded edge of the fabric as close to the zip teeth as you can. Repeat on the second piece of fabric. Leave your zip partially open so you can open it fully once it has been sewn together.

6 Using a sewing machine (or a needle and thread) stitch the zip in place securely.

7 With the zip closed three quarters of the way, pin the cushion back and the finished Bargello pieces together with right sides facing. Take your time to make sure everything lines up.

8 Stitch around all four edges to attach the back and front pieces together.

9 Trim the seam allowances and snip the corners diagonally as close to the stitches as you can.

10 Slide the partially open zip all the way open and turn the cushion the right way out. Use closed scissors to push the corners out into neat points.

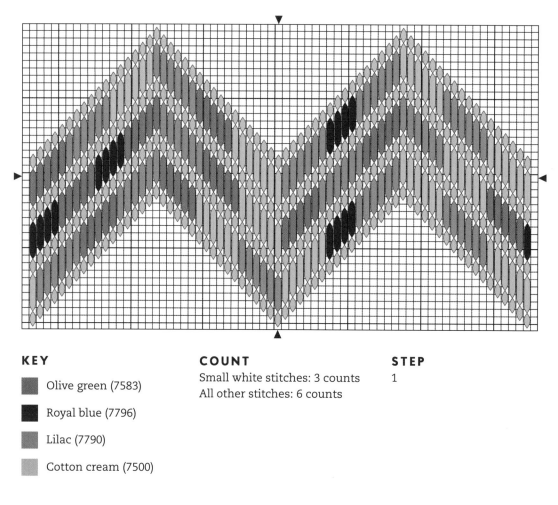

KEY

■ Olive green (7583)

■ Royal blue (7796)

■ Lilac (7790)

■ Cotton cream (7500)

COUNT
Small white stitches: 3 counts
All other stitches: 6 counts

STEP
1

Flower cushion

SKILL LEVEL  10 HOURS +

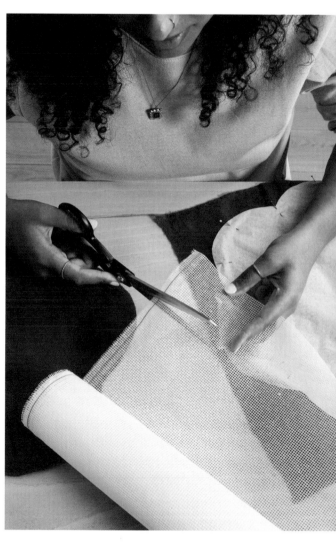

A Bargello book would be nothing without some retro flower power. This modern take on a classic 70s symbol is finished in luxe, rust velvet. There's just a hint of Bargello to finish the edge and give a subtle nod to decades past.

PATTERN
Scallop

MATERIALS
10-count tapestry canvas
DK yarn in 3 colours
Size 18 tapestry needle
50cm (20in) of velvet furnishing fabric
Polyester fibrefill
2 x 4cm (1⅝in) self-covered buttons

SKILLS
Stitching with tapestry canvas
Following a pattern
Creating a filled cushion

METHOD

1 Draw a circle with a 42cm (16½in) diameter on a piece of paper. Using a ruler, mark the centre. Then use the centre spot as a guide, draw a line through the centre of the circle, dividing it in half. Divide each half into three segments and draw connecting lines, so the entire circle is split into six segments.

2 Using a pencil, mark 22cm (8¾in) in from the outer circle on each divider line, then mark 10cm (4in) outwards from the top of the divider line on each side.

3 Join these two points together with a curved line to create the petal shapes. Try to make these curves as even as possible. Cut out your template twice so you have two flower shapes on paper.

4 Cut a piece of paper 125x7cm (49x2¾in) for the gusset strip.

5 Pin the flower templates onto the wrong side of the velvet fabric and cut around them neatly. Pin the long paper template to your tapestry canvas and cut this neatly too. If necessary, you can cut two pieces of canvas and join them together.

6 Stitch your Bargello panel using the chart on page 96. Leave a 1cm (⅜in) seam allowance all around so you can easily attach the canvas to your flower cushion pieces.

7 Use a sewing machine (or a needle and thread) to join the ends of your canvas panels together, so you have a loop filled with Bargello stitches.

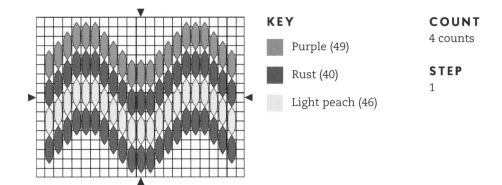

KEY

■ Purple (49)

■ Rust (40)

■ Light peach (46)

COUNT
4 counts

STEP
1

8 Lay one of the flower panels on a flat surface with the right side facing you. With the right side of the canvas facing the flower panel, begin pinning the Bargello piece to the edges of the flower. You will need to work with the curve of the flower, so use lots of pins and don't be afraid to pin and re-pin to make it perfect.

9 Using a sewing machine or a needle and thread, sew the pinned pieces together. Go with the curve of the flower to ensure it keeps its shape in the final project.

10 Once complete, repeat the same process with the second flower panel. This time when pinning and sewing, leave a 5cm (2in) turning gap – this will be hand finished after you fill the cushion.

11 Using the tip of an iron, gently press open the seams and then turn the cushion the right side out, pulling the bulk through the turning gap.

12 Piece by piece, tear off small amounts of filling and insert them into the opening of the cushion. Fill the cushion evenly for a nice, plump finish.

13 Once you're happy the filling is evenly distributed, take a needle and matching colour thread and neatly sew the seam closed.

14 Following the manufacturer's instructions, cover your buttons using velvet fabric scraps.

15 Thread a needle with matching thread and stitch a button to one side, directly in the middle of the cushion. Pull the needle through to the centre of the opposite side of the cushion pulling it tightly to create a tufted effect. Make sure the button is firmly in place, and then tie off the thread.

16 Add the other covered button to the other side of the cushion, covering the stitching from the button that is already in place.

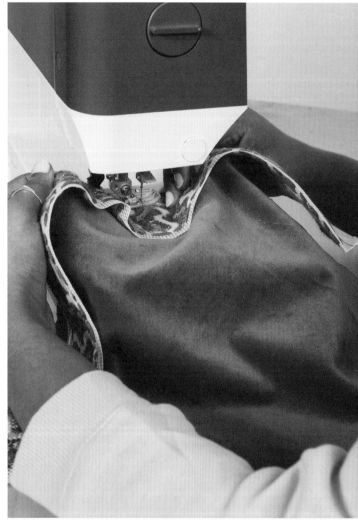

Tote bag

SKILL LEVEL

 5 HOURS +

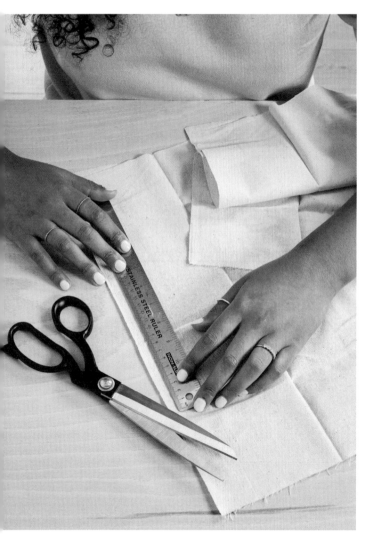

Add some personality to your humble cotton tote bags and learn about the wonders of soluble canvas with this project. Keep it simple using just one colourway, or add more shades and yarn textures for a more detailed look.

PATTERN
Diamonds

MATERIALS
14-count soluble canvas
DK yarn in 1 colour
Size 18 tapestry needle
Cotton canvas 1m (1yd)
Leather bag straps
Pinking shears

SKILLS
Stitching with soluble grid
Following a pattern

METHOD

1 Pre-wash a piece of cotton canvas fabric. To avoid creasing, remove the fabric from the machine and dry flat.

2 Once dry, lay a towel on an ironing board and place the canvas on top. Set your iron to the cotton setting, then use a spray bottle to mist the fabric in sections. Iron both sides of the canvas to steam it dry.

3 Once the fabric is crease-free, cut it to 38x84cm (15x33⅛in).

4 Using a piece of chalk, measure down 10cm (4in) from the top of the canvas and make a mark. Then from here, measure a further 1cm (⅜in) and make another mark. This is going to be your stitch line.

5 Take your sheet of soluble canvas and cut it to the desired width. This project uses an 8x38cm (3⅛x15in) piece for the top panel. Cut the sheets to size and pin them onto the bag. Use a lot of pins as the canvas will shift around as you stitch.

6 Thread a needle and begin stitching the pattern over the canvas following the chart on page 102, being sure not to pull the stitches too tight as you go.

7 Once you've completed your pattern, fill a bowl with hot water and immerse the stitched section of the fabric in it. Leave it to soak for 10 minutes, moving occasionally.

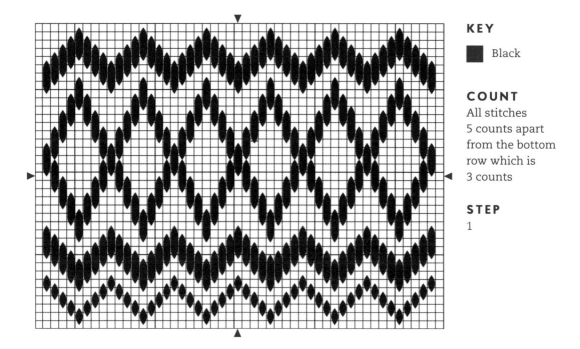

KEY

■ Black

COUNT
All stitches
5 counts apart
from the bottom
row which is
3 counts

STEP
1

8 After 10 minutes, remove the canvas from the bowl and run it under a gently running tap, carefully rubbing your finger over where the soluble canvas was until it's all gone. Avoid getting all of the fabric wet if you can, so you won't have to iron the whole piece again.

9 Go back to the ironing board and press any of the canvas that got wet to remove the creases. Fold the canvas in half, pressing a crease on the bottom half. Press in the 10cm (4in) and 1cm (⅜in) lines you drew on both sides of the canvas.

10 Now we're going to add the straps to the bag. Using a pencil, mark the holes in the straps onto the panel in your desired position. Then create a hole in the panel, and attach the straps following the manufacturer's instructions.

11 Fold over the 8cm (3⅛in) panel so it covers the back of your stitches and the section where you attached the handles.

12 Fold under the 1cm (⅜in) allowance and pin the section in place. Neatly sew a straight line across the edge of the seam, using the bottom of your pattern as a guide.

13 Place your bag fronts right sides together and stitch along the sides.

14 Using a pair of pinking shears, trim the seam allowance down by half.

15 Turn the bag the right way out using a point turner or the sharp tip of your closed scissors to make sure the corners are nice and sharp. Press the edges so they are crisp.

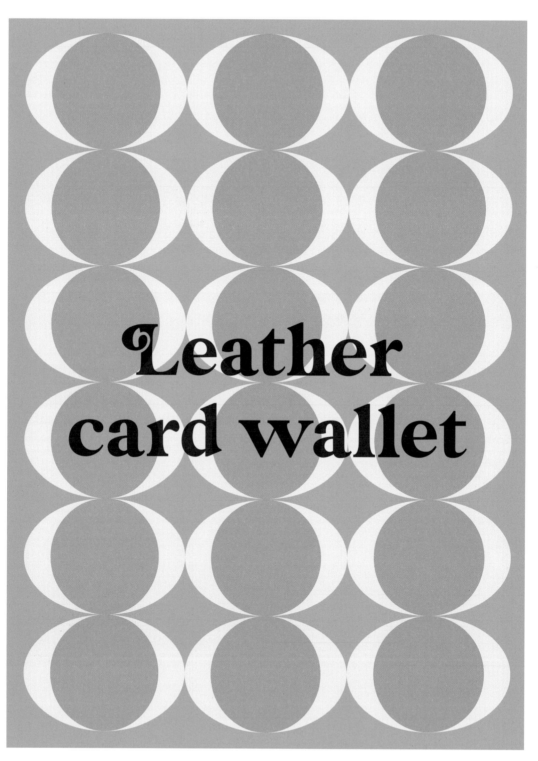

Leather card wallet

SKILL LEVEL    3 HOURS

This project is equal parts practical and stylish. Once again we'll use an alternative material as our canvas. Perforated leather is traditionally used in car repair, purchase a small amount to create a leather card wallet.

PATTERN
Hungarian Point

MATERIALS
Perforated leather 9.5x6cm (3¾x2⅜in)
4-ply yarn in 3 colours
Size 18 tapestry needle
1.2mm (¼in) perforated and plain leather
Bulldog clip

SKILLS
Stitching with alternative materials
Following a pattern
Working with leather

METHOD

1 To get started on this project, we'll create a paper template. Take a card from your wallet and trace around it, adding a 5mm (¼in) seam allowance. This will ensure you'll be able to take your bank cards in and out. Stitching on leather will warp it slightly, so creating a template will ensure the holes match up when sewn.

2 Cut out your template, and then lay it on your perforated leather. Use a bulldog clip to keep the template in place and then cut around it with a sharp pair of scissors. Repeat to cut out a matching piece of plain leather for the back of the wallet.

3 Stitch your Bargello pattern onto the perforated leather following the chart below, ensuring you leave the set of holes closest to the edge empty so you can stitch the two pieces together.

4 Once your design is complete, use a needle and thread to stitch the two pieces together. Don't forget to leave an opening for your cards!

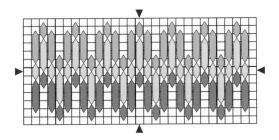

KEY

■ Peony pink (038)

■ Pearl (043)

■ Green beryl (077)

COUNT
Alternating 5 counts
with 3 counts

STEP
1

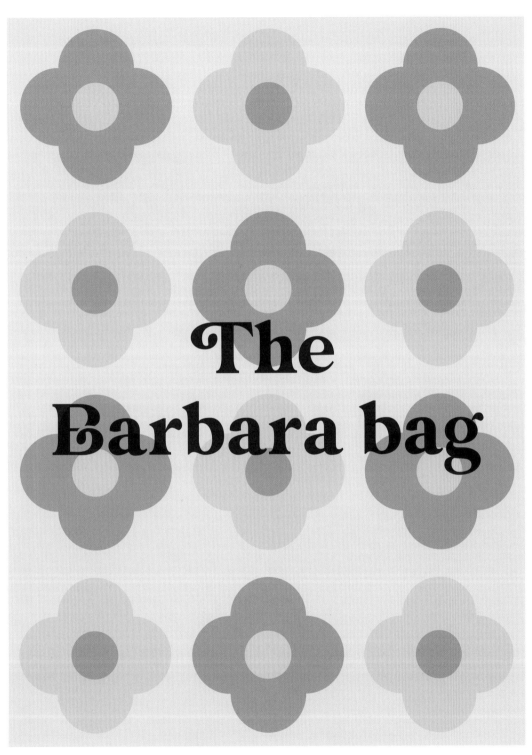

The Barbara bag

SKILL LEVEL    **10 HOURS +**

Inspired by the ornate bags that can be seen on the catwalks of London and Paris, the Barbara bag is perfect for day or night. Not only does Barbara have stud feet so you can put her down anywhere without fear of ruining your stitching, she also has D-rings so you can switch out the handles as you please!

PATTERN
Flowers

MATERIALS
10-count plastic grid
Tapestry wool in 3 colours
Size 18 tapestry needle
4 bag stud feet
2 bag handles of your choice
Fabric for bag lining (optional)
4 d-rings

SKILLS
Stitching with plastic canvas
Following a pattern
Building a structure

METHOD

1 Cut your panels to size using the following measurements and quantities:

- 2 x side panels: 9.5x18cm (3¾x7⅛in)
- 2 x front panels: 18x18cm (7⅛x7⅛in)
- 1 x bottom panel: 18x9.5cm (7⅛x3¾in)

2 Following the chart on page 112, stitch the repeat on all of your canvas pieces, leaving one row of squares empty at the top of each side, front and back panels.

3 Following the manufacturer's instructions, attach the stud feet to the bottom panel of the bag. You may need to snip out a stitch or two to push these through the holes. On your bottom panel, make a mark to show where you'll push the stud feet through and skip these stitches. You may need to use a scalpel or scissors to remove some of the grid here so leaving out the stitches for a few squares in this area will really help with this process.

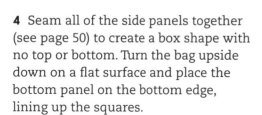

4 Seam all of the side panels together (see page 50) to create a box shape with no top or bottom. Turn the bag upside down on a flat surface and place the bottom panel on the bottom edge, lining up the squares.

5 Stitch the bottom panel in place by looping your threads around the edges.

6 Optional: To line your bag, cut lining fabric pieces the same size as your main panels. Use a sewing machine (or a needle and thread) to stitch the pieces together using a 1.5cm (⅝in) seam allowance. Fold over the top edge of the assembled lining by 1cm (⅜in) and stitch this edge to the empty row of squares you left free of stitches.

7 Once you have created the bag outer (and the lining if applicable), edge stitch all around the top of the bag (see page 55), adding two D-rings to the left-and right-hand sides of each front panel. Make sure the handles are in the same position on each side of the bag.

8 Add your handles, and your Barbara bag is ready to go!

COUNT
White flower (from left to right):
Row 1: 3 counts
Row 2: 4 counts
3 counts at the centre

Pink flower (from left to right):
Row 1: 3 counts
Row 2: 5 counts
Row 3: 4 counts
3 counts at the centre

Blue background colour:
5 counts

STEP
1

KEY

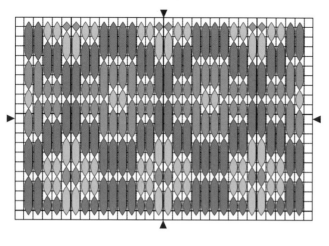

■ Grey (7284)

■ Beige (7500)

■ Lilac (7284)

>> **7** <<

Upcycled collar

SKILL LEVEL   5 HOURS +

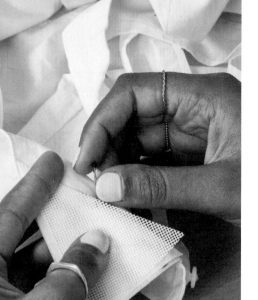

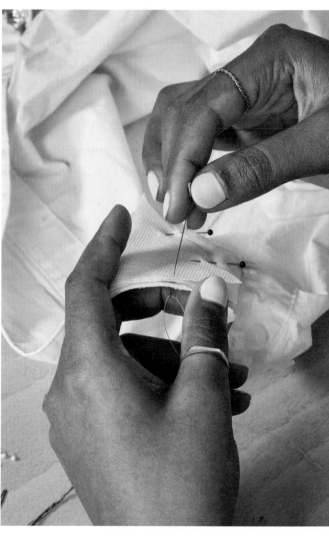

Breathe some new life into an old garment using beads to add a touch of sparkle. This thrifted shirt uses a combination of delicate stitches and freestyle beading.

PATTERN
Zig zag

MATERIALS
14-count tapestry canvas
Stranded cotton in 1 colour
Beads (various)
Beading needle
Cross-stitch needle

SKILLS
Stitching with stranded cotton
Beading
Upcycling a garment

METHOD

1 Start by deciding on the area you want to embellish. Place a piece of paper on top of this area so you can trace the rough shape.

2 Cut out the template shape out and pin it to your tapestry canvas. Cut around the template with a pair of scissors.

3 Once you have your pieces cut, pin them to your shirt collar. Use lots of pins here so that the canvas doesn't shift as you stitch.

4 Using a beading needle, start by laying a foundation you can follow with stitches. Rod-shaped beads can be staggered to create a faux Bargello zig zag stitch.

5 Come up through the canvas, place your bead on the needle, and then come back through just above where the bead naturally lays. Pull the needle through to stitch the bead securely in place. Repeat until your first row is full.

6 Next, use a slightly sharper cross-stitch needle and stranded cotton to add a row of zig zag stitches in stranded cotton above and below the beading following the chart on page 118. These stitches will give you a guide to follow with more beads.

7 Continue stitching until the area is filled. Remember, this technique is all about experimentation and having fun, so you don't need to be too precise when adding beads.

8 As you get to the edges of your canvas, stitch over the canvas slightly to hide the edges and make everything look neat and tidy.

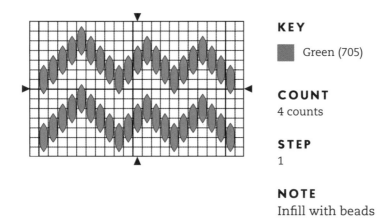

KEY

■ Green (705)

COUNT
4 counts

STEP
1

NOTE
Infill with beads

>> **7** <<

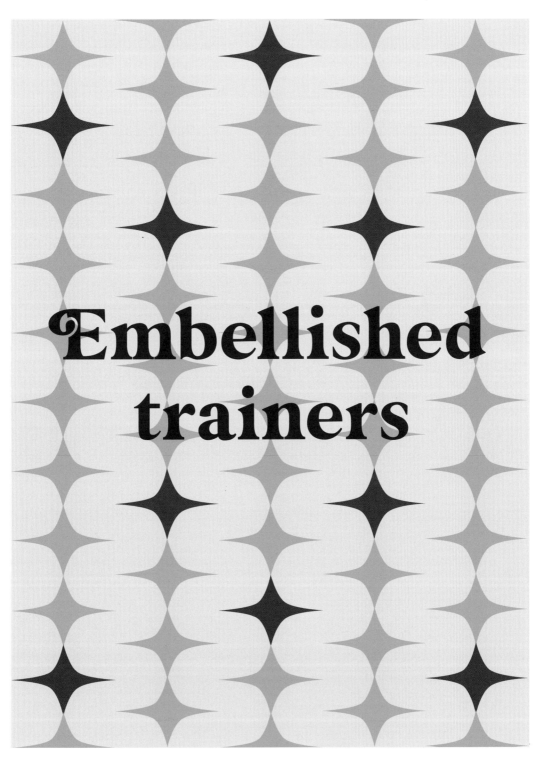

Embellished trainers

SKILL LEVEL   5 HOURS +

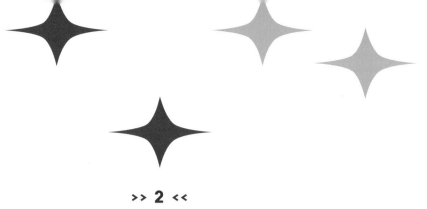

>> **2** <<

>> **4** <<

Add a spring in your step and some colour to a blank canvas with this easy upcycling project. Once you see your design come together, there will be no shoes in your wardrobe safe from Bargello stitch!

PATTERN
Chevron

MATERIALS
10-count tapestry canvas
Tapestry wool in 4 colours
Size 18 tapestry needle
Blank pair of canvas trainers

SKILLS
Stitching on an alternative canvas
Upcycling a garment

METHOD

1 Decide on the area you want to stitch onto and place a piece of paper on top so you can trace the rough shape.

2 Cut out the template and pin it to your tapestry canvas. Cut around the template with a pair of scissors.

3 Pin the tapestry canvas to your trainers so you can begin stitching. Use lots of pins so that the canvas doesn't move as you stitch.

4 Now it's time to stitch your design using the chart above. Come up through the trainer fabric and the tapestry canvas and then back through, continue until the repeat design is complete.

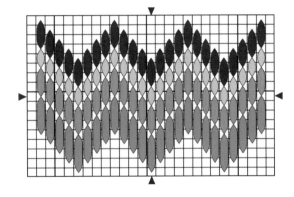

KEY

■ Burgundy (7157)

■ Beige (7500)

■ Pink (7605)

■ Beige pink (7221)

COUNT
From top to bottom:
Row 1: 4 counts (burgundy)
Row 2: 3 counts (cream)
Row 3: 4 counts (pink)
Row 4: 5 counts (dusky pink)

STEP
1

Upcycled jacket

SKILL LEVEL **III** 10 HOURS +

Personalization is a great way to turn a bargain charity shop find into the garment of your dreams. This project adds simple, geometric Bargello stitches to a plain denim jacket so you can really make your mark on a thrifted piece.

PATTERN
Triangles

MATERIALS
14-count soluble canvas
Acrylic yarn in 1 colour
Size 18 tapestry needle
Denim jacket

SKILLS
Stitching on an alternative canvas
Upcycling a garment

METHOD

1 Mark out your stitching area on the jacket using chalk or a removable pen. Cut your soluble canvas to size and pin it in place. Use lots of pins as this material will shift a lot as you stitch – you may also need to butt together more than one sheet of canvas.

2 Begin stitching your repeat onto the jacket following the chart. To make sure the canvas doesn't move around too much, try and do this on a flat surface.

3 Following the manufacturer's instructions, soak the soluble canvas off of the jacket. As it won't be possible to undo this, make sure the design is perfect before you begin.

4 You may want to handwash the jacket in warm soapy water to remove any residue from the canvas.

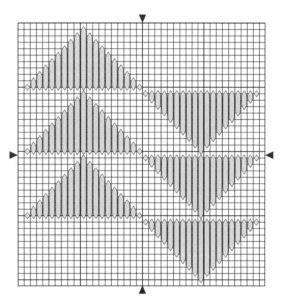

KEY

▨ White

COUNT
Form a triangle by starting with 2 counts and working up to 11 counts. Then work back down from the centre point

STEP
1

Letter patch

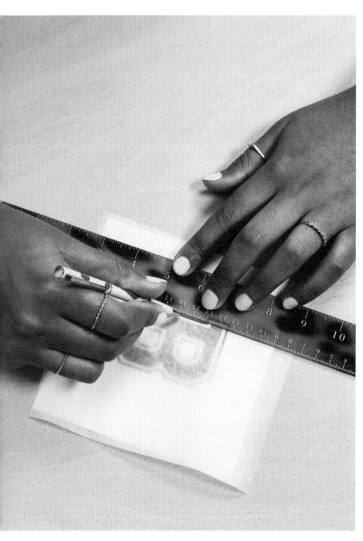

The personalization trend isn't going anywhere, and these letter patches are a great way to make your mark on your favourite garment. Choose a single letter, or spell out a word or slogan to make a punchy statement!

PATTERN
Chevrons

MATERIALS
14-count tapestry canvas
Stranded cotton in 5 colours
Cross-stitch needle
Stiff felt
Iron-on adhesive

SKILLS
Stitching with stranded cotton
Following a pattern
Customizing garments

METHOD

1 To begin, draw your design out on a piece of paper. If it helps, you can type your letter on your computer, print it out, and trace around it.

2 Take a piece of 14-count canvas and trace your template onto it using a washable pen. Where possible, if your letter has straight lines, try to line these up with the grid.

3 Trace your template shape onto the felt, adding 5mm (¼in) around all edges. Cut out.

4 Layer the canvas letter over the felt letter, ensuring the 5mm (¼in) border is even on all sides.

5 Now you can begin stitching following the chart on page 132. It helps to lay your patch over the pattern and make some markings first, so you know which colours and stitch lengths go where. If your pattern jumps across the canvas, simply shorten or lengthen your stitches to fit them on the letter.

6 Fill your letter to the edge. For the rows closest to the felt border, stitch just over the grid to ensure the edge of the canvas is neatly hidden.

7 Cut a piece of iron-on adhesive roughly to the size of your letter. Using a dry iron, fuse it to the back of your patch.

8 Trim the adhesive to the edge of the border, so all the pieces are the same size.

9 To attach the patch to your sweater, pin it in place and try the garment on to make sure you're happy with the positioning. Take the sweater off and iron from the inside to fuse the bonding.

10 Leave the patch to cool. Your garment is ready to wear!

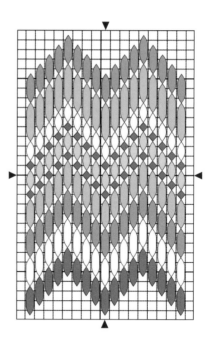

KEY

▪ Orange/pink (21)

▪ Dark purple (155)

☐ White (27)

▪ Deep orange (22)

▪ Purple (211)

COUNT

From the top down:
Row 1: 4 counts
Row 2: 5 counts
Row 3: 3 counts
Row 4: 2 counts
Row 5: 3 counts
Row 6: 2 counts
4 counts for everything
that remains

STEP

1

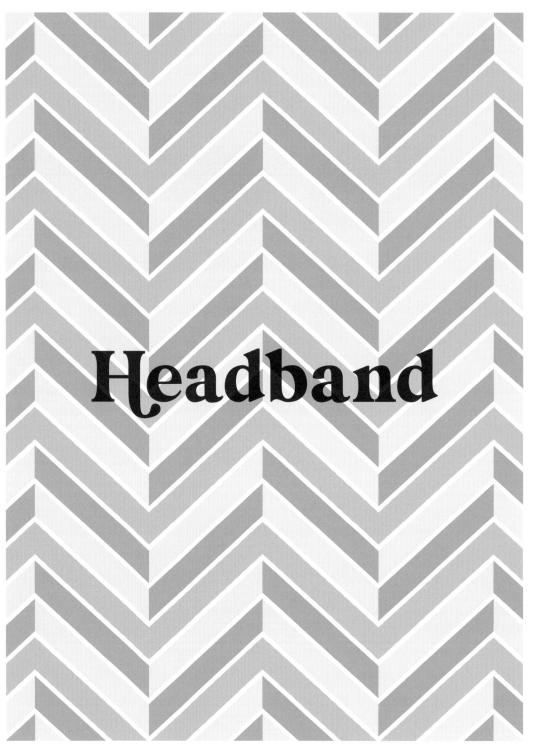

Headband

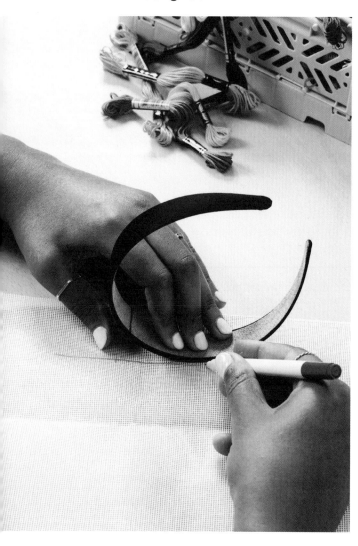

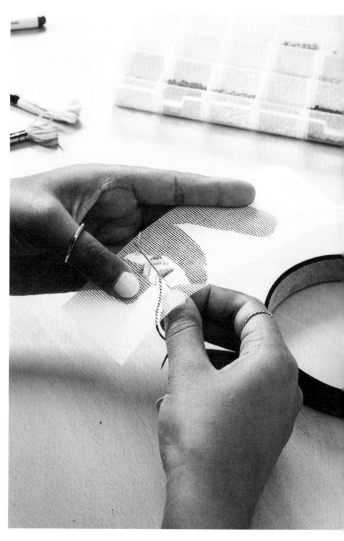

You can never go wrong with a statement hair accessory and what better statement to make than with some colourful Bargello. Upcycle an old headband or breathe some life into a plain one with this project.

PATTERN
Chevrons

MATERIALS
7-count tapestry canvas
Stranded cotton in 3 colours
Cross-stitch needle
Headband blank
Glue gun/double-sided tape
Ric rac braid or ribbon (optional)

SKILLS
Stitching with stranded cotton
Following a pattern
Customizing garments

METHOD

1 Mark the centre spot on the underside of your headband blank.

2 Take a piece of canvas and place the centre section of the headband on top, making sure there is enough canvas on both sides to cover the band. Then mark the centre spot on the canvas.

3 Take a soluble marker and gently roll the headband to one side, marking the canvas on both sides as you go. When you get to the end, draw a line to show the end of the headband. Roll it back to the middle and repeat on the other side. Once you have traced the shape, remove your headband and mark a 1cm (⅜in) seam allowance around all edges of your lines.

4 Begin stitching the design, keeping your threads inside the template as much as possible to reduce unnecessary bulk.

5 When you've completed your pattern, lay the canvas right side down on a flat surface.

6 Using a glue gun or strong double-sided tape, cover the surface of the headband blank, then line it up with the centre mark you made earlier.

7 Roll the headband onto the canvas to bond the two securely. Finish the edges with glue or tape, then fold them to the underside of the band.

8 Optional: To neaten the underside of the headband, cover the folded canvas edges with some ric rac braid or ribbon.

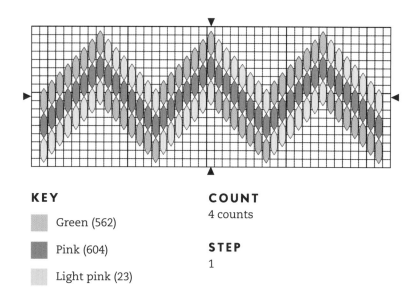

KEY

■ Green (562)

■ Pink (604)

■ Light pink (23)

COUNT
4 counts

STEP
1

Resources

Below I have listed the specific materials I used for each project, which you can refer to when making the projects for yourself.

PLANTER COVER (PAGE 46)
❯ 10-count plastic grid
❯ DMC tapestry wool in:
  Tan (7453), Yellow (7058), Orange (7436),
  Light pink (7151), Dark pink (7605)
❯ Size 18 tapestry needle

TRINKET DISH (PAGE 53)
❯ 10-count plastic canvas
❯ DMC tapestry wool in:
  Peach (7853), Beige (7173), Coral (7852)
❯ Size 18 tapestry needle
❯ Pre-drilled 15cm (6in) wooden base
  from Fred Aldous

UPCYCLED LAMPSHADE (PAGE 58)
❯ Wool & The Gang 'Ra-Ra Raffia' in: Coal
  Black and Cinnamon Dust
❯ Darning needle from Hobbycraft
❯ Lampshade from Made.com

WALL HANGING (PAGE 63)
❯ 10-count plastic grid (full sheet)
❯ DMC tapestry wool in:
  Beige (7500), Orange (7436),
  Dark pink 7605
❯ Size 18 tapestry needle
❯ Wooden macramé dowel
  from Hobbycraft

FRAMED WALL ART (PAGE 70)
❯ 10-count plastic grid
❯ Paintbox Yarns Simply DK in:
  Granite grey (106), Melon sorbet (116),
  Vintage pink (155)
❯ Size 18 tapestry needle
❯ Pine deep box frame 20x20cm
  (8x8in) from Hobbycraft

UPCYCLED FURNITURE (PAGE 77)
❯ Wool & The Gang 'Ra-Ra Raffia' in: Ivory
  white, Desert palm
❯ Darning needle from Hobbycraft

SQUARE CUSHION (PAGE 80)
❯ 7-count tapestry canvas from
  Stitcher.co.uk
❯ Stylecraft Special Chunky in:
  Pale rose (1080), Mustard (1823),
  Teal (1062), White (1005)
❯ Size 18 needle
❯ Cushion back velvet curtains
  from IKEA
❯ 42cm (16½in) zip from Hobbycraft

OBLONG CUSHION (PAGE 87)
❯ 10-count tapestry canvas from
  Stitcher.co.uk
❯ DMC tapestry wool in:
  Cotton cream (7500), Lilac (7790)
  Olive green (7583), Royal blue (7796)
❯ Size 18 tapestry needle
❯ Cushion back velvet curtains
  from IKEA
❯ 42cm (16½in) zip from Hobbycraft

FLOWER CUSHION (PAGE 92)

❯ 10-count tapestry canvas from Stitcher.co.uk
❯ DK yarn from Hobbii.co.uk in: Purple (49), Rust (40), Light peach (46)
❯ Size 18 tapestry needle
❯ Pattern paper from Fred Aldous
❯ Stuffing for cushion from Hobbycraft

TOTE BAG (PAGE 99)

❯ 14–count soluble canvas from Hobbycraft
❯ Knitcraft Black Everyday DK Yarn from Hobbycraft
❯ Size 18 tapestry needle
❯ Cotton canvas fabric from Hobbycraft
❯ Handles from Fred Aldous

LEATHER CARD WALLET (PAGE 104)

❯ Perforated leather from eBay
❯ Yarn and Colours Must-Have (Minis) in: Peony pink (038), Green beryl (077), Pearl (043)
❯ Size 18 tapestry needle
❯ Leather back from 'Leather Needle Thread'

THE BARBARA BAG (PAGE 109)

❯ 10-count plastic grid from Hobbycraft
❯ DMC tapestry wool in: Beige (7500), Lilac (7790), Grey (7284)
❯ Prym bag feet
❯ D-rings from Hobbycraft
❯ Bag handles from eBay
❯ Lining fabric from Minerva.com

UPCYCLED COLLAR (PAGE 114)

❯ 14-count tapestry canvas
❯ DMC stranded cotton in: Green (912)
❯ Cross-stitch needle
❯ Beading needle

EMBELLISHED TRAINERS (PAGE 121)

❯ 10-count tapestry canvas from Hobbycraft
❯ DMC tapestry wool in: Beige pink (7221), Burgundy (7157), Pink (7605), Beige (7500)
❯ Size 18 needle

UPCYCLED JACKET (PAGE 124)

❯ 14-count soluble canvas from Hobbycraft
❯ Knitcraft White Everyday DK Yarn from Hobbycraft
❯ Size 18 tapestry needle

LETTER PATCH (PAGE 129)

❯ 14-count tapestry canvas
❯ DMC stranded cotton in: White (27), Purple (211), Dark purple (155), Orange/Pink (21), Deep orange (22)
❯ Cross-stitch needle
❯ Stiff felt from eBay
❯ Heat'n'Bond Ultra Hold Iron-On Adhesive from Hobbycraft

HEADBAND (PAGE 134)

❯ 14-count tapestry canvas from Hobbeycraft
❯ DMC stranded cotton in: Light pink (23), Pink (604), Green (562)
❯ Cross-stitch needle
❯ Headband blank from eBay

Acknowledgements

Just one page in this book truly isn't enough to thank all of the people that supported me to make this book happen. I'm eternally grateful to everyone in my life for every message, zoom call, voice note and pep-talk. If you're reading this I hope you know how much it meant to me to have you in my life, whilst I disappeared into my spare room to write. It has been a labour of love and I'm so proud of every single stitch, every project and every page in this book. Now I have the feeling back in my thumbs after all that stitching, there are definitely some people I owe an extra special shout out too.

Firstly, to Matt, my partner, my best friend and my rock – you always believe in me, even when I don't believe in myself. Thank you for spurring me on, never letting me quit my dream and for not being mad at me for finding yet another tapestry needle nestled in the living room rug. I owe you all of my success and I hope one day I can repay you for pushing me forward and helping me to create my greatest achievement to date. I love you.

To my little sister Mica, (the only person with thumbs as sore as me) for being a willing stitcher in my time of need. And for always doing it with enthusiasm and a sense of humour, sometimes into the early morning. Your spirit was infectious as I wrote this book and I can't thank you enough for being a part of the Bargello Gang.

To my Editor, Harriet, for believing the world needed a book of modern Bargello projects and for entrusting me to be the person to bring that vision to life. For your patience, kindness and most of all your belief throughout this project – I'll never forget the day your email

FIND ME ONLINE
@nerrisapratt | @thebargelloedit
www.thebargelloedit.com

Share your makes me online
by tagging #bargelloedit

with the subject 'Bargello Book' popped up into my inbox and changed my life forever, thank you a million times over.

To the team that were so instrumental in taking the vision I had in my head and translating it into visuals far more eloquently than I ever could:

Katherine Keeble, for her incredible design work and Bargello inspired illustrations that bring so much colour to these very pages. Sarah Hogan for not only letting us take over her home but for her expertise and kindness guiding me through the shoot, when I truly had no idea what I was doing with my hands or my face. Charlotte Love for not only giving me the chance to collaborate with someone who's work I've admired for such a long time, but for being a wealth of knowledge when it came to styling my babies (aka my Bargello projects). And of course, Gary Blake, videographer extraordinaire for shouting Chapelle show quotes at me to keep my spirits up and always sharing my creative visions even when I can't eloquently put them into words (which is always).

And to those of you who don't even know you had an impact. Holly James, my personal cheerleader who kept my business running whilst I stitched my heart out. You're a truly incredible human being and I owe you so much. Tabara N'diaye, fellow author and friend, who was so kind and giving with your advice at all points during the book writing process, I can't thank you enough.

And last but not least, to my parents Jon and Yvonne who from a young age have always pushed me to use my creative brain and my hands to create beautiful things. Mum, I'm so grateful to have you to bond with over a joint love of art and design and craft. I hope you know that without your talent and skill to always inspire me, I wouldn't be the crafty person I am today. Dad, I know you don't have a crafty bone in your body and as such you have no idea what I'm doing half the time, but I hope that when you look at this book, it reminds you of the day we met, me 3 or 4 years old in my little pink fluffy dressing gown showing you my craft projects. I love you both so much.

And finally, to every single person who has supported The Bargello Edit since its launch. Your support, purchases and advocacy have been the creative fuel I needed to create each and every project in this book – this one's for the #BargelloGang.

Publishing Director Sarah Lavelle
Senior Commissioning Editor Harriet Butt
Design and Art Direction Katherine Keeble
Prop Stylist Charlotte Love
Photographer Sarah Hogan
Head of Production Stephen Lang
Senior Production Controller Katie Jarvis

Published in 2021 by Quadrille,
an imprint of Hardie Grant Publishing

Quadrille
52–54 Southwark Street
London SE1 1UN
quadrille.com

Cataloguing in Publication Data: a catalogue
record for this book is available from the
British Library.

Text and projects © Nerrisa Pratt 2021
Photography © Sarah Hogan 2021
Design © Quadrille 2021

ISBN 978 1 78713 725 7
Printed in China

I would like to extend a special thank you
to the brands that gifted tools, materials
and props for the shoot.

Hobbycraft | hobbycraft.co.uk
Fred Aldous | fredaldous.co.uk
Jasmine Flowers | jasmine-flowers.co.uk
Pico. the store | picothestore.com
Mayflower Bespoke |
mayflowerbespokejewellery.co.uk
Feather & Nest | featherandnest.co.uk
DMC | dmc.com/uk
Ilk and Ernie | ilkandernie.com
Florence London | florence-london.com
PFAFF | pfaff.com